My Favorite Superhero

By Stephanie Unale & Amanda Kunkel

TRUE LIGHT ✝ BOOKS

Dedication

Without question, we thank God for His endless love, guidance, and grace throughout every step of this journey. This book is dedicated to our father, Charles "Chikk" Myers, for none of this could have happened without him. Thank you for believing in us and our dreams. Also, to our Aunt Sheri Leigh Myers, whose keen eye and thoughtful edits turned these words into something truly special. And to our husbands and children, for your love, support, and patience—you are our inspiration.

Copyright

This book, My Favorite Superhero, and all images and text herein are copyright © 2024 True Light Books. Reproduction in whole or part is strictly prohibited without express written permission from the authors.
True Light Books is a joint venture between Stephanie Unale and Amanda Kunkel, with editorial and project management assistance from Sheri Leigh Myers.

ISBN 979-8-218-52804-1

Hi! I'm Beth.
I am a star that lives
way up in the sky.

I can see everything
from up here, all over the world.

Genesis 1

I've been up here a long time so I have seen many, many people.

But there is One who is the greatest person who has ever lived.

Matthew 5:1-2

And you know what?

He became the greatest Superhero of all time!

John 8:12

His name was Jesus.
He was sent from Heaven by God
who gave Him His superpowers.

Let me tell you all about Him...

Matthew 5:1-2

God wanted to show Jesus' birth was special. God made me shine the brightest I have ever shone...

...because Jesus is the Son of God.

John 8:12

Like when Jesus was about your age, he walked to the market with his mother Mary to trade some yarn for flour.

As they were leaving the market, Jesus saw a family in a small hut who did not have any food.

Hebrews 13:16

Even when Jesus was little, he always knew the right thing to say and do.

Jesus asked his mother for some of the flour and shared it with the poor family so they could bake bread to eat and sell.

Matthew 25:34-40

As Jesus grew up, he learned from his earthly father Joseph how to be a carpenter. He learned how to build and repair things like furniture and houses.

He used these skills not only for work but also to help others.

1 Thessalonians 5:15

Like when Jesus was hurrying home, he found a traveler along the road with a broken cart.

Jesus stopped to fix it so the traveler could continue on his way.

Acts 20:35

When God decided it was time, Jesus was *baptized*. Jesus went into the water and had his head dipped under to show he would follow God.

Then light shone down from Heaven and God filled Jesus' heart with what is called the "Holy Spirit."

Matthew 3:13-17

He was blessed with *special powers!*

One time, when some fishermen returned to the shore after not catching fish all night, Jesus told them to cast their net one more time.

Luke 5:5-6

The fishermen were tired but they went back out and cast their net anyway. When they did, their net was overflowing with fish.

Jesus used His superpowers given by God for good, like to heal people!

Matthew 8:14-15

When someone was sick, He could lay His hands on them and make them all better.

Jesus also used His superpowers to feed people.

Like when He was talking to a very large crowd of people and they had very little food to eat.

Jesus turned the little bit of food into lots of food and fed everyone!

Matthew 14:13-21

Jesus spoke to many people about God and how we should live our lives based on love and forgiveness.

Matthew 12:14

But, some people did not believe that His superpowers were real and that He was the Son of God. It made them so angry they decided to crucify Jesus.

Jesus went through something very painful called the Crucifixtion.

He was nailed to a wooden cross by His hands and feet and left to die.

We were heartbroken.

This was all a part of God's plan.

Sometimes there may be a lot of sadness before God's miracles can happen.

John 3:16

God's biggest miracle is called the *Resurrection.*

God gave Jesus the superpower to come alive again!

Matthew 28:1-4

It showed the world that Jesus spoke the truth about God and was right about how we should live.

John 20:11-18

Jesus now lives in Heaven with God
way up in the sky,
past the moon and the stars.

His superpowers are even *greater* now.

1 Peter 3:22

He can now be anywhere and everywhere, with anyone, all at the same time!

Jesus' greatest superpower is how much He LOVES you!

All you have to say is "Jesus come into my heart" and he will.

Proverbs 3:5-6

Jesus never gets mad or stops loving you no matter what you do or what you say.

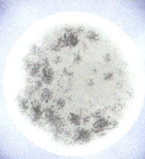

His love is SO powerful you can *feel* it.

Jeremiah 29:12-13

You can talk to Jesus about *anything*.

If you are having a bad day or feeling scared, you can put your hand on your heart.

Joshua 1:9

Close your eyes, take a deep breath and say "Jesus".

He will help you feel better.

Romans 15:13

So that is how Jesus came to be the GREATEST SUPERHERO of all time!

1 John 5:14

Talk to Jesus whenever you need, He *understands*, loves you *SO* much, and is *always* there to help.

"For the Kingdom of God belongs to those who are like these children."

Luke 18:16

Discussion Questions:

What are some of Jesus' superpowers?

Prompt: Giving, Healing, Multipling Food, and Loving Us.
He can also be anywhere and everywhere at once.

Where does Jesus live?

Prompt: Heavens, Everywhere, in our Hearts

What do we do when we want to talk to Jesus?

Prompt: Get quiet, Place our hands on our hearts,
Say his name.

What are some nice things that you can do to help people?

Superhero Lift Off – Mindfulness and Connecting to Jesus

Alright, let's use our superpowers to help us be calm and kind like Jesus!

Now stand up tall! Put on your superhero cape with a big *whooshing* sound.

When I say "Go" march your feet as fast as you can as I count to ten! *Go!*

Now place your hand here on your chest. What do you feel?
You feel your heart beating? That is where Jesus Christ lives!

He is always with you and you can always talk to Him, even though you cannot see Him. Jesus is always there to listen.
His love and understanding is the superpower that helps us feel calmer, especially when we feel really angry or sad.

Parents/Teachers:

Practice consistently to build your child's connection to calm and Jesus, calling on the His superpower of love. Prayer and meditation helps calm our children's brains and improves their learning and self regulation. For a deeper dive, check out our online course:
Loving Discipline based on Your Child's Brain Development:
lovingdisciplineparenting.com

ACTIVITY PAGE

CAN YOU FIND BETH?

She is somewhere on almost every page! Can you draw a picture of Beth?

LET'S FIND THE LAMBS!

What do lambs say? What color are they? Did you know Jesus is called the Lamb of God?

LET'S FIND THE DOVE!

What pages do you see the dove on? Did you know the dove is a symbol of the Holy Spirit?

WHERE ARE THE BASKETS?

Can you count the baskets? What happened with the baskets? Jesus did something amazing! After feeding over 5,000 people with just a little bit of bread and fish, there was still so much food left. 12 whole baskets of food! It was a miracle that showed how much Jesus cares for us and provides what we need.

WHERE IS THE CROSS?

What happened on the cross? Jesus loved us so much that He did something really brave, like a Superhero. He gave His life so that we could be saved and live happily with God forever.

EXPLORING THE SCENE - LEARNING MORE

MARKET

Where do we go to buy our food? In Jesus' time they did not have refrigerators, so people had to go to the market almost every day. What happened when Jesus went to the market and saw the poor family? What differences do you see from the left to right page?

FISHING

Some people's jobs were to fish so they could sell them in the market. Do you like to eat fish? Did you know that Jesus and his friends ate a lot of fish? What happened with Jesus and the Fishermen?

NATIVITY

What is a manger? Can you name all the animals? Why is Beth important at Jesus' birth? Because she is the Star of Bethlehem! Three wise men followed Beth's bright shining light to worship Jesus when He was born.

Scripture

"Then Christ will make his home in your hearts as you trust in him. Your roots will grow down into God's love and keep you strong. And may you have the power to understand, as all God's people should, how wide, how long, how high, and how deep his love is. May you experience the love of Christ, though it is too great to understand fully. Then you will be made complete with all the fullness of life and power that comes from God."
~ Ephesians 3:17 - 19

When you believe in Jesus, it's like He moves into your heart to stay with you. His love is super strong, like big roots that help a tree stand tall. Jesus loves you so much that it's even bigger than anything you can imagine! His love fills your heart completely, like how a glass gets filled all the way up with water. His love is so big, it's wider than the sky, longer than the biggest road, higher than the tallest mountain, and deeper than the ocean! When you know how much Jesus loves you, it helps you feel happy and safe inside, no matter what happens.

Nighttime Prayer

Thank you Jesus for what you've done.
Thank you God for giving your son.
Now Jesus is a friend of mine.
He hears my prayers at any time.
It may be dark, but I will not fear.
I know in my heart He is always near.
Bless my family and all those I love
and send your protection from up above.
Amen

~Stephanie Unale

Stephanie (writer) lives in Arizona with her husband and two boys. She draws inspiration from her personal journey with Jesus and her desire to create stories that capture children's attention. She believes that portraying Jesus as a young boy can help children connect and inspire them to be kind and thoughtful. Her goal is to create more books that use Jesus as an example to teach children about mindfulness and emotional well-being through positive lessons.

Amanda (artist) currently lives in Georgia and has been happily married to her husband for 17 years. Together, they have three children. She has always believed in Jesus and has a beautiful testimony about falling away and coming back to Jesus. This book marks her first experience bringing her artwork to life on a computer. The result is beautifully showcased in this book. Amanda plans to continue creating children's books and exploring digital art.

The sisters are excited about the many ideas they have in the works and look forward to bringing more stories to life for young readers.

Follow along with Stephanie and Amanda's journey at
http://myfavoritesuperhero.com
or by following them on Instagram
@Jesusmyfavoritesuperhero
@truelightbooks